WHAT THE

BIBLE SAYS ABOUT

DR. DAVID R. REAGAN

DR. THOMAS H. BAKER

Dedicated to

Phillip

an AIDS victim who died in the Lord

All scripture quotations are from
the New American Standard Version
© The Lockman Foundation

Illustrations by Jack Hamm

Copyright© 1988 by Lamb & Lion Ministries

LAMB
&' LION
MINISTRIES
P. O. Box K
McKinney, TX 75069
ISBN Number 0-945593-00-7

Printed in the United States of America

Cover design by Richard Slaton

Typographical design by Perry Printers in Columbus, Indiana

TABLE OF CONTENTS

77324

A BIBLICAL PERSPECTIVE ON THE AIDS PLAGUE

By Dr. David R. Reagan

I was called of God in 1980 to preach the soon return of Jesus. In my preaching on this vital subject, I emphasize what I call "the signs of the times" which I believe point to the Lord's soon return. I divide the signs into six categories — the signs of nature, society, religion, technology, world politics and Israel.

The Signs of Nature

I have found that the category of signs which carries the least respect is the one pertaining to nature. It is the category that includes such natural phenomena as earthquakes, famine, pestilence and "signs in the heavens." (See Matt. 24:7 and Luke 21:11.) We in the western world tend naturally to scoff at such signs because we are too rationalistic to believe that God would ever speak to us supernaturally through some catastrophe like a tornado or a hail storm. Yet the Bible is full of examples of God doing exactly that.

In the book of Joel the prophet tells the people of Judah that the locust invasion that has stripped their fields bare was sent by God to call them to repentance. He warns that if they do not repent, God will send something worse — an invading army (Joel 1:13-2:13). They turned deaf ears to the message, and God sent the Babylonians to take them into exile. God likewise warned the nation of Israel through the prophet Amos. Amos told the people that all the natural calamities they had suffered — drought, wind storm, mildew, locusts, pestilence and famine — had been sent by God to bring them to repentance (Amos 4:6-13). The people never seemed to learn or remember the lesson. After the Babylonian captivity, the descendants of those whom Joel and Amos had preached to lapsed into the sins of their forefathers. God raised up another prophet, Haggai, who told them that they would suffer a drought sent by God until they repented. (Haggai 1:1-11).

Another reason people tend to scoff at the signs of nature is because such signs have always been with us. "We've always had famine and earthquakes — what else is new?" This attitude ignores the statement of Jesus recorded in Matthew 24:8 where He said the natural signs would be like "birth pangs." That means they will increase in frequency and intensity as we near the time of His return. In other words, there will be more earthquakes and more intense ones; more famine and more intense famine; more signs in the heavens and more intense ones. It sounds like the evening news on television.

The Sign of Pestilence

But what about pestilence — that is, epidemic disease? It has been the most difficult sign of all to get people to pay attention to. The very idea of pestilence increasing in frequency and intensity has been laughable to most people. We have smugly assumed that our high-tech medical science had everything under control and could easily conquer any new disease that might develop.

In thinking this way we ignored the fact that medical science still has a long way to go to solve the mysteries of the two major killers — heart disease and cancer. We also ignored the fact that old diseases we thought we had conquered are coming back strong with new strains that are resistant to our antibiotics. For example, the Center for Disease Control in Atlanta reported early in 1987 that a penicillin resistant strain of gonorrhea has now spread to the point that "talk of eradicating it may be impractical." The number of reported cases of the new strain in the U.S. jumped 90% in 1986 over the number reported the year before.

As the decade of the 80's began, people laughed at the idea of new, incurable diseases emerging which could confound medical science and raise once again the horrible spector of epidemics. No one is laughing now. The Sexual Revolution has spawned Herpes Simplex II, an incurable veneral disease afflicting heterosexuals. And it has produced Acquired Immune Deficiency Syndrome (AIDS), an incurable, deadly disease afflicting homosexuals. As AIDS now spreads from homosexuals to drug abusers to prostitutes and on to the general population, we stand on the precipice of a dark abyss. We face the deadliest epidemic since the Black Plague in the 1300's which killed one-fourth of the population of Europe. We face an unprecedented *pandemic* — an epidemic of world wide proportions that has the potential to kill hundreds of millions.

The Facts about AIDS

The first cases of AIDS to be reported in this country to the Center for Disease Control were diagnosed in 1981. Since the virus has a long incubation period that can last up to ten years, it is believed that the virus entered this country in the early 70's.

The virus itself (called HIV for Human Immunodeficiency Virus) was not isolated and identified until 1984. It was originally named "GRID" for Gay Related Immunodeficiency Disease. It was given this name because over 90% of the originally diagnosed cases were among male homosexuals. The name was later changed to AIDS due to extensive lobbying by homosexual political groups.

The AIDS virus causes the collapse of the body's immune defenses by severely reducing the number of white blood cells. The afflicted person usually dies of the secondary infections which the body can no longer fight. The most common cause of death is pneumonia. Another is a rare form of cancer called Kaposi's sarcoma.

The virus is unique in medical history. It is a type referred to technically as a "retro-virus" and is the first retro-virus ever to be discovered in human beings. Previously such viruses were known to afflict only animals. It resembles the viruses that produce bovine leukemia, infectious anemia in horses, and goat encephalitis. No cures for such diseases have been developed, and the afficted animals are usually slaughtered.

Since the virus is the type found previously only in animals, some experts believe it mutated from a similar green monkey virus found in Central Africa where tribal

3

rituals often mingle human and animal blood. It is theorized that the virus was carried by Central Africans to Haiti and that Haitian male prostitutes infected vacationing homosexual men from New York City.

The virus is unique in another respect. It is a "slow motion" virus. That means it has a long incubation period, usually four to seven years. Because of this characteristic, it is really impossible to determine how many people are already infected by the virus without testing everyone. The slow incubation period is offset by the rapid progress of the disease once the symptoms begin to manifest. Eighty per cent die within 18 months of the time the disease is diagnosed.

Another unique characteristic of the virus is that it has a chameleon quality in that it mutates rapidly, constantly developing new strains. This is one of the characteristics that makes it next to impossible to develop a vaccine.

The virus is hardy. It can survive outside the body for periods as long as ten to fifteen days, even in a dry state.

The only confirmed methods of transmission are sexual intercourse, the sharing of intravenous needles among drug users, mother to fetus during pregnancy, and exposure to contaminated blood by transfusion. However, there are unexplained cases. And the virus has been found in body fluids such as saliva, tears, breast milk, urine and mucus.

Not all infected persons develop AIDS. It was originally estimated that 30% of those infected would develop a full blown case. That estimate has now been raised to 50% and may go higher as more is learned about the disease. Some infected people develop what is called Aids Related Complex (ARC). They suffer some of the symptoms but not all. Any carrier of the virus can transmit it to others.

The Grim Statistics

As of January 1988 there had been 50,262 confirmed cases of AIDS reported in the U.S. Over 28,000 of these had already died. The number of actual cases is certainly larger than these official figures. The reason for the underreporting is due to the social stigma of the disease. Since the AIDS victim dies of secondary infections like pneumonia, it is easy to cover up the real cause of death. The attempt to do this with the death of Liberace is an example of the problem.

Eighty countries world wide have reported AIDS cases to the World Health Organization. The numbers they have reported are highly unreliable because of the social stigma attached to the disease. In fact, some African countries, where the infection rate is estimated to be 20% of the population, refuse even to submit reports. Official estimates place the number of infected Africans at five million, double the number in the U.S. The World Health Organization estimated in 1987 that there had been 100,000 cases in the world since 1981, that there were currently ten million infected people, and that there will be 100 million infected people world wide by 1990.

Although the disease began in this country among homosexual men, it has spread to other groups. Still, as of 1988, it continues to be primarily a homosexual disease. This is a fact that is covered up in the media reporting due to pressure from homosexual lobbying groups.

The facts speak for themselves regarding this issue. At the end of 1987, 73% of all diagnosed cases in the U.S. were among homosexual men between the ages of 20 and 50. This group composes only 2% of the entire population! The next largest group of infected persons were intravenous drug users. They constituted 17% of the diagnosed cases. Seven per cent of the cases were among babies born to infected mothers. Three per cent had contracted the disease from blood transfusions.

The grim statistics of the AIDS epidemic become overwhelming when you consider the implication of the virus' long incubation period. The New York Medical College at Valhalla estimates that two million Americans are already infected with the virus. These are people who are currently healthy because they have not yet manifested any symptoms of the disease. Most are not even aware that they are carriers of the virus. They are walking time bombs, infecting other people.

Since it is believed that the infection rate is growing exponentially by doubling annually, it is estimated that 25% of our population will be infected within five years. That means that by 1992 we will have 64 million infected people in the U.S. alone, with over 300,000 diagnosed cases.

U.S. AIDS Statistics
(Based on CDC Projections)

Year	Estimated Number Infected (Not Diagnosed)	Confirmed Cases
1987	2,000,000	50,000
1988	4,000,000	91,000
1989	8,000,000	136,000
1990	16,000,000	194,000
1991	32,000,000	268,000
1992	64,000,000	375,000

The cost estimates that have been matched to these statistics are staggering. In the U.S. it is estimated that it will cost $40 billion in 1992 just to house those who are dying of AIDS. It is also estimated that we will run out of hospital beds in that same year.

Consequence or Judgment?

As the enormity of the horror of AIDS sinks in, more and more people are beginning to ask a basic theological question. They want to know if this pandemic is a natural consequence of immorality or is it a judgment of God?

I believe that it is both. Certainly it is a consequence of immoral behavior. The Bible says you can be assured that "your sins will find you out" (Num. 32:23). The same truth is expressed in the New Testament in a different way: "Do not be deceived. God is not mocked; for whatever a man sows, this he will also reap" (Gal. 6:7).

The alcoholic has no one to blame but himself for his cirrhosis of the liver. The smoker who contracts lung cancer is simply reaping what he has sown in bodily abuse.

But the Bible also makes it clear that God will tolerate a multiplication of sin only so long before He will intervene and pour out His wrath in judgment. The idea of a wrathful God judging nations or groups for sin is patently offensive to some people, even many Christians. But it is very Biblical.

God is not the great "Pussy Cat in the Sky" who winks at sin. He destroyed the whole earth with water because "the wickedness of man was great" and "every intent of the thoughts of his heart was only evil continually" (Gen. 6:5). He utterly devastated the cities of Sodom and Gomorrah because of their rampant immorality. He delivered Israel into the hands of the Assyrians. He condemned Judah to captivity in Babylon. He poured out His wrath on Jerusalem in 70 AD and scattered the Jews all over the world. The earth is littered with the rubble of once great nations who were swept into the dust bin of history by the judgment of God. These events are a reminder of the words of the prophet Nahum:

> The Lord is avenging and wrathful.
> The Lord takes vengeance on His adversaries,
> And He reserves wrath for His enemies.
>
> (Nahum 1:2)

The American Apostasy

The tragic truth is that our nation has become an enemy of God. We have called the wrath of God down upon our heads because we have allowed sin to multiply. We sowed a "sexual revolution" in violation of God's Word, and we are reaping the consequences.

God's Word makes it clear that the only moral sex is sex within the marriage relationship between husband and wife. By contrast, society says, "If it feels good, do it!"

First came the heterosexual revolution. It happened fast. In my lifetime I can remember when a top Hollywood actress had to end her career and move to Europe because it was revealed that she was living with a man to whom she was not married. Such a public reaction to immorality today is unthinkable. "We've come a long way, baby" in a very short time, and it's all been in the wrong direction. Today you can flip on the Johnny Carson show and watch interviews of stars and starlets who openly brag about being "AC & DC" (that is, bisexual) or homosexual or lesbian. Even those who are "straight" seem compelled to make it clear that they are "with it" as far as the sexual revolution is concerned — so they go out of their way to emphasize that they are not married to the person they are living with.

As the sexual revolution gained momentum, it began to promote itself through the radical feminist movement and through the glorification of immoral sex in movies, television, music, and magazines. "Abortion on demand" became the rallying cry of the revolution, and we began to sacrifice our babies on the altar of feminism.

Increasingly, an assault was made on the basic unit of Western civilization — the family. Marriage was held up to open contempt. The "liberation" of the homemaker was idealized. Divorce became epidemic.

The Church also became an object of scorn as society

rapidly secularized. Efforts were made to isolate the influence of the Church. "Separation of Church and State" became the slogan of the day, and a Humanist dominated Supreme Court jumped on the band wagon, implementing the slogan into law, despite the fact that it is found in the Soviet Constitution and not our own.

All religious influence was removed from our public schools, and the American educational process was delivered into the hands of God hating Humanists who were determined to suppress the truth about the origins of Man and the universe. Our schools quickly disintegrated into battle grounds between undisciplined children and indulgent educators.

Our whole society began to slide into a moral morass of lawlessness, juvenile delinquency, alcoholism, drug abuse, venereal disease, pornography and corruption in high places. Humanism replaced Christianity as our national religion. Materialism became our God. Greed became our motivator. Hedonism became our national lifestyle as we became caught up in an obsessive pursuit of pleasure. And the payoff of all this flight from God has been despair — the kind Paul prophesied would characterize the end time society:

> In the last days . . . men will be lovers of self, lovers of money, boastful, arrogant, revilers, disobedient to parents, ungrateful, unholy, unloving, irreconcilable, malicious gossips, without self-control, brutal, haters of good, treacherous, reckless, conceited, lovers of pleasure rather than lovers of God.
>
> (II Tim. 3:1-4)

The Homosexual Revolt

As the wave of immorality grew in force, it was only a matter of time before it would express itself in a demand for approval of the ultimate sexual perversion — homosexuality. Gradually at first, and then with increasing militancy, the homosexuals began to come out of the closet and flaunt their perversion before the media, marching through the streets celebrating the "Gay" lifestyle and demanding legal protection of their terrible sin.

As the homosexuals have grown in boldness and political effectiveness, the government, the media and the church have stood paralyzed before them. Spineless politicians and public health officials have been afraid to take any action that might be construed as "anti-Gay." In the process they have converted AIDS into the first political disease in history.

Instead of taking decisive action to close AIDS spawning grounds like homosexual bath houses and requiring quarantine of all AIDS victims — as has been done in the past with similar victims of epidemics — the politicians have actually focused their energies on passing legislation to protect AIDS victims from any kind of discrimination, including insurance coverage. AIDS has thus emerged as the first deadly disease in history to have civil rights! It's as if our constitution gives a Typhoid Mary a legal right to contaminate society. Such ridiculous thinking is a measure of the perverseness of our values. We call evil good and good evil (Isa. 5:20).

Like the government, the media have been intimidated by the militancy of the homosexuals. Television networks have submitted programs to homosexual groups for preview to make certain that nothing objectionable to their lifestyle is aired. News reports on the epidemic have down played the danger of infection and have refused to acknowledge that AIDS is basically a homosexual plague. Political rallies by homosexuals have been given maximum coverage, while those opposing them have been ignored.

A 1987 PBS television program on AIDS presented a classic example of the media bias. Called "AIDS: Changing the Rules," it was promoted as an educational program for heterosexuals — as if heterosexuals are the problem. It was hosted by Ron Reagan, son of President Reagan. The whole show focused on "safe sex," including a demonstration of how to wear a condom, using a banana as a prop. Reagan concluded the show with these words: "AIDS is not a moral issue. You don't get AIDS because you're bad or do bad things. You get AIDS because you're unlucky." May God have mercy on us!

Actually there is much more than intimidation involved in the media's favorable response to the homosexuals. Opinion polls have shown for a long time that the American media are firmly in the grasp of Humanists who favor the sexual revolution and who are determined to protect every aspect of it, including the freedom of homosexuals to flaunt their perversion and spread their disease.

Worse yet has been the reaction of the Church. Instead of standing upon the authority of God's Word and speaking out boldly against the sodomites who are polluting our society — the Church has caved in to the sin, muttering platitudes like "God hates the sin but loves the sinner." Or, worse yet, many professing Christian leaders, caught up in apostasy, have shamelessly endorsed the sin, arguing that the Bible really does not condemn homosexuality. Some churches have even ordained practicing homosexuals, making a mockery of God's Word. Explicitly homosexual churches have even been established whose purpose is to assure sodomites that they need not repent of their sin to be accepted by God.

The bottom line is that our society has been sliding into a moral sewage pit for the last thirty years. And the sexual revolution is only a part of the picture. We call ourselves a "Christian nation." That's a mockery. We lead the world in every abomination known to man — alcoholism, drug addiction, pornography, child abuse, juvenile delinquency, crime, divorce — you name it.

To compound the situation, we are exporting our immorality to the rest of Mankind. All over the world our TV programs and movies that glorify violence and sex are being shown to hundreds of millions. We are the prime moral corrupter of planet Earth.

The Noahic Precedent
"There is nothing new under the sun" (Eccl. 1:9). Other

11

civilizations have had their sexual revolutions which led to moral chaos and ultimate collapse. The Bible chronicles one of those collapses in grisly detail — the society of Noah's day. Keep in mind that Jesus said He would return at a time when society would once again be in the miserable state that characterized the days of Noah (Matt. 24:37).

From the Old Testament we learn very little about Noah's society except that it "was corrupt in the sight of God" and was "filled with violence" (Gen. 6:11). The wickedness was deeply rooted because the Word says that the people of that day were continually obsessed with evil thoughts (Gen. 6:5). Jesus characterized the society as a spiritually insensitive one. Despite the constant preaching of Noah in which he warned the people of God's wrath and called them to repentance, the people went about their business "eating and drinking, marrying and giving in marriage," seemingly oblivious to the impending doom (Matt. 24:38). They laughed and scoffed at Noah, and some continued laughing until they could tread water no longer. Hearts were hardened against God.

The most detailed description of Noah's degraded society is contained in Romans chapter one. In verse 18 it says that the society suppressed the truth about God in unrighteousness — even as we have done in our own society by refusing to allow the truth about the origins of Man and the universe to be taught in our public schools. Because they suppressed the truth about God, we are told in verses 23 and 25 that they worshiped the creation rather than the Creator. In like manner, our society has given itself over to a Humanistic philosophy that exalts Man rather than God.

We are then told that because they "exchanged the truth of God for a lie" (verse 25), "God gave them over in the lusts of their hearts to impurity" (verse 24). It's as if the Lord stepped back and lowered the hedge of protection around them and allowed evil to multiply. The result was a sexual revolution that led to a wave of immorality in which they "dishonored their bodies" (verse 24).

In verse 26 we are told that God took another step back and lowered the hedge even more. Because they chose to wallow in immorality, we are told that "God gave them over to degrading passions" (verse 26). An epidemic of homosexuality broke out. "Women exchanged the natural function for that which is unnatural" (verse 26). And in the same way, "men abandoned the natural function of the woman and burned in their desire toward one another, men with men committing indecent acts" (verse 27).

It is at this point that the passage in Romans chapter one reveals something very interesting. It says that when the people turned to homosexual activity, they "received in their own persons the due penalty of their error" (verse 27). Note that statement carefully. What it's saying is that AIDS, or something like it, has been around before!

The outbreak of homosexuality seems to have been the final stage in the moral deterioration of Noah's society. The outbreak itself is pictured as a judgment of God upon the society because of its overall ungodliness.

The Judgment of God

In like manner, God has judged our society by allowing an epidemic of homosexuality. And God, in turn, is judging the homosexuals with the epidemic of AIDS.

To picture these calamities as judgments of God really bothers many Christians. Some do not believe in the wrath of God. To them God is the "Cosmic Teddy Bear" who is warm and soft and winks at sin. Such a God would never hurt a fly. I have already shown that image to be patently false. God's holiness and righteousness require Him to deal with sin. Look again at the passage we have been studying in Romans. It begins in Romans 1:18 with the words, "For the wrath of God is revealed from heaven against all ungodliness and unrighteousness of men."

Others are repulsed by the idea of AIDS being a judgment of God because they point out that it affects a small percentage of "innocent" people like babies and blood transfusion recipients. But that argument ignores three things.

First, there is no such thing as a truly "innocent" person. We are all born with a sin nature. Second, we live in a fallen world where the "innocent" often suffer from the sins of others. Child abuse is a classic example. Finally, the argument ignores the fact that the "innocent" have always been affected by the wrath of God — as when He destroyed the earth with water, destroyed Sodom and Gomorrah with fire, and devastated Judah with a locust invasion.

To paraphrase an observation made by Billy Graham: "If God is not judging us for our homosexuality, then He needs to apologize to Sodom and Gomorrah."

The Sin of Homosexuality

The Church will never come to grips with AIDS until it first of all musters the moral courage to denounce the sin that has brought the judgment. The reluctance to do so is a classic example of apostasy, for the Word of God makes it crystal clear that homosexuality is a stench in the nostrils of God.

There are church leaders who argue that the Bible does not condemn homosexuality. That is sheer nonsense. Homosexuality is condemned as a sin against God in both the Old and New Testaments. It was one of the sins for which Sodom and Gomorrah were destroyed. (Gen. 19:1-29). It was specifically singled out in the Mosaic law as "an abomination" (Lev. 18:22). In fact, the Mosaic law prescribed the death penalty for homosexual activity (Lev. 20:13). In the New Testament, Paul wrote: "Do you not know that the unrighteous shall not inherit the kingdom of God? Do not be deceived; neither fornicators, nor idolaters, nor adulterers, nor effeminate, nor homosexuals, nor thieves, nor the covetous, nor drunkards, nor revilers, nor swindlers, shall inherit the kingdom of God" (Romans 6:9-10).

Many humanist Christian leaders have tried to explain away these scriptures as they have attempted to endorse homosexuality as an "alternative lifestyle." They have also attempted to justify the ordination into the ministry of practicing homosexuals. These religious leaders are caught up in spiritual darkness. They are the type referred to by Paul when he wrote: "Though they know God's righteous decree that those who do such things deserve death, they not only continue to do these very things but also approve of those who practice them" (Rom. 1:32).

Verses 'Gay' Ministers Cut from the Book

These deluded Christians usually argue that the Old Testament expresses superstition about homosexuality and that the New Testament expresses Paul's personal prejudice. These arguments, of course, reveal their basic rejection of scripture as being inspired by the Holy Spirit (II Tim. 3:16). They then add insult to injury by asserting that homosexuality couldn't be all that bad because Jesus never condemned it. What a pitiful argument! That's like saying there's nothing wrong with child molestation, incest, or bestiality because Jesus never specifically condemned these sexual perversions.

The fact is that Jesus had a lot to say about sexual

morality, and what He had to say clearly rules out homosexuality as an acceptable lifestyle before God. In Matthew 19:1-9 Jesus taught that all sexual unions must be judged in reference to God's original intention and not in terms of human opinion and desire. And Jesus proceeded to point out that God's original intention was that "a man shall leave his father and mother and be joined to his wife, and the two shall become one flesh."

The "Gay" Lifestyle

Many people really do not understand what homosexuality is all about. It has been idealized by both the homosexuals and the media as simply an "alternative lifestyle" or "gay lifestyle." The super liberal National Education Association recently issued a teaching unit for our public schools that portrayed homosexuality as "normal." In fact, the unit said that "being homosexual is like being left handed."

SODOMY

Gay
Homosexual
Alternative Lifestyle

Condoning Words
to mask perversion

This willful
progression
of rebellion against God
is begging judgment
for our land!

Repent
and He
will forgive!

Kay Hedger

Satan is very clever and very deceitful. The reality about homosexuality is anything but "normal." It is certainly not "gay." That is a mockery of language. Nor is it an "alternative lifestyle." No, it is an alternative death style.

Let's take an in-depth look at the wretchedness of this "lifestyle" that so many are laboring to glamorize. I want to warn you in advance that the picture is not pretty. It is loathsome and repulsive.

The May 1985 issue of the *American Journal of Public Health* reported a survey of sexual activities among 655 homosexual males living in San Francisco, a city where five people are dying daily of AIDS. The men were specifically asked about their sexual activities during the past thirty days. Here are the results:

1) Every person admitted having had sex with strangers. The total encounters ranged from 2 to 10 strangers.
2) Five per cent reported they had drunk the urine of a lover.
3) Thirty-three per cent had experienced oral-anal contact.
4) Fifty-three per cent had injested semen.
5) Fifty-nine per cent had received semen in the rectum.

The Institute for the Scientific Investigation of Sexuality reports:

1) Two-thirds of homosexuals regularly lick and/or insert their tongue into the anus of their partners.
2) More than one-third participate in "fisting" — that is, the insertion of the hand into the rectum of a lover.
3) Thirty per cent participate in "golden showers." This is where one person urinates on the other.
4) Thirty-seven per cent admitted participating in some form of sado-masochism (torture).
5) Ninety per cent admitted to illegal drug use.
6) Seventeen per cent said they had either eaten or rubbed themselves with the feces of a partner!

17

Gay? The old derisive term, "Queer," seems more appropriate.

The same study showed that the average homosexual has oral sex with 106 different men in a year's time and experiences 72 penile penetrations of the anus. Most encounters took place in either bath houses or public restrooms. Eighty-eight per cent admitted to having taken part in a group orgy, and 46 per cent said they had participated in sexual acts with minors. The Kinsey Report estimated that the average homosexual has 1,000 sexual partners in a lifetime. The *Village Voice* estimates it as being closer to 1,600.

A Personal Encounter

Such outrageous promiscuity reminds me of a conversation I once had with a homosexual. The man called me in response to a radio broadcast I had made on the subject. He asked if he could meet with me and talk with me personally about his problem. We arranged to meet for lunch at a cafeteria in a downtown Dallas office building.

The man turned out to be a 35 year old CPA who was working as an accountant for a major corporation. He was married and had two young daughters. He had what most people dream of — a good education, an outstanding job, and a beautiful family. Yet, he was miserable, for he was in bondage to homosexuality.

Not knowing much then about the practice of homosexuality, I asked him how he made his sexual contacts. "Oh, that's easy," he responded. "I just go to a public restroom in one of these downtown office buildings each day at lunch time and wait around for a contact. It never takes long."

"You mean you just have sex with anyone who comes along — with total strangers?" I asked.

"Yes," he responded, "and sometimes with as many as three during one lunch break."

He explained that he hated himself and his double life. With tears in his eyes, he asked, "Is there any hope for a person like me?"

The Only Hope

Is there any hope for the homosexual? The world says the only hope is for homosexuals to stop thinking of themselves as being perverted or sinful. They are to accept themselves as they are and rejoice in their "difference" by calling themselves "Gay." The world's solution is no solution at all. The homosexual is still left with the guilt and emptiness of his unnatural existence.

There *is* hope for the homosexual, but it is not to be found in glorifying the sin. The one and only true hope for the homosexual is Jesus Christ. Through the power of His Spirit, the homosexual can be delivered from bondage to his sin, either by receiving complete deliverance from his perverted lust or by receiving the power to control the lust.

The most encouraging message any homosexual could ever be given is the one contained in the Word of God in I Corinthians 6:9-11. I call this passage a bad news/good news message. It begins with terribly bad news, but it ends with incredibly good news. The bad news is Paul's assertion that homosexuals can not inherit the kingdom of God. The good news is found in the next sentence. Paul writes: "And such were some of you, brethren. But you have been washed, sanctified and justified in the name of the Lord Jesus Christ and by the Spirit of God."

Isn't that marvelous? Those words were addressed to saved children of God. Paul says, "such were some of you." Yes, some of the Christians at Corinth had been sexual perverts, but they had been delivered from their bondage by the power of God in Christ Jesus. Hallelujah!

AMAZING PARALLELS
BETWEEN DEUTERONOMY 28
AND THE AIDS EPIDEMIC

by Dr. Thomas H. Baker

The book of Deuteronomy consists of a series of speeches delivered by Moses to the Children of Israel on the plains of Moab as they prepared to enter the Promised Land. A generation had died in the wilderness after forty years of wandering. In these speeches Moses sought to orient the new generation to their covenant relationship with God.

In his first speech (chapters 1-4), Moses reviews the history of their wilderness wanderings and exhorts them mightily to avoid idolatry. In his second speech (chapters 5-26), Moses surveys the general requirements of their covenant with the Lord (chapters 5-11) and then presents a detailed exposition of the principal laws of that covenant (chapters 12-26). Moses next gives directions for a ceremony for the covenant's renewal that was to be followed when Israel entered the Promised Land (chapter 27). As chapter 28 opens, Moses turns his attention to the blessings of obedience and the curses of disobedience which the covenant promises the people.

Warnings of Judgments

If Israel obeys the Lord, then every aspect of the nation's life will be blessed (28:1-14). But just as obedience will bring blessings, so disobedience will bring curses (28:15-68). The curses are presented as judgments from the Lord. A great variety are named such as blight, scorching heat and drought, defeat in battle, physical and mental disease, oppression, loss of material goods, exile, economic ruin, crop failure, etc. Each individual judgment is presented as having one basic goal — to turn sinners from disobedience.

The reasons for the judgments are repeated over and over in this short section· of scripture (28:15-68). Verse 15 states these curses will be the consequence of disobedience, resulting from the people's failure to obey the Lord and do all His commandments. These judgments are presented as certain, and it is stated that the curses will come upon them and overtake them "on account of the evil of your deeds, because you have forsaken me" (verse 20).

Again in verse 45 the Lord says all these curses will come on them and overtake them until they are destroyed, if they do not obey the Lord their God by keeping His commandments and His statutes. Verse 58 repeats this same theme, underscoring the fact that they should be careful to observe all the words of the law and "fear this honored and awesome name, the Lord your God." Finally, verses 59 and 62 again repeat that the major portion of the population will be wiped out through extraordinary plagues if they do not obey the Lord their God.

Plagues in Prophecy

These prophecies of Moses that God will punish sin with plagues are not the only such prophecies in the Bible.

God warned the nation of Judah repeatedly through Jeremiah and Ezekiel that the people's sins would result in a judgment of pestilence if they did not repent (Jer. 14:12 and Ezek. 5:12). Amos pointed out to the nation of Israel that their rebellion against God had resulted in a plague (Amos 4:10). When King David angered God with his unauthorized census which reflected his trust in manpower rather than the Lord, the prophet Gad told him that he and his nation must suffer judgment. David was given a choice of famine, pestilence or military defeat. David chose pestilence, and the resulting plague killed 70,000 people (II Sam. 24:15).

The New Testament also contains prophecies that God will punish sin with epidemic disease. One example is found in Revelation 2:18-29 where Jesus sends a message of condemnation to the immoral apostate church at Thyatira. The letter clearly shows how God views and deals with sexual immorality. The church was promised a judgment which would cause her to suffer intensely: "Behold, I will cast her upon a bed of sickness, and those who commit adultery with her into great tribulation, unless they repent of her deeds" (verse 22). In verse 23 the Lord adds, "I will kill her children with pestilence; and all the churches will know that I am He who searches the minds and hearts; and I will give to each one of you according to your deeds." Note that the promised judgment for immorality is pictured as a dramatic illness that will result in intense suffering and will also cause the death of their children.

In His Olivet Discourse (Matt. 24 and Luke 21), Jesus prophesied that the society of the end times would be one characterized by the same immorality that prevailed in Noah's time (Matt. 24:37), and He also prophesied that the end time society would be afflicted with plagues (Luke 21:11). According to Revelation 6:8, early in the Great Tribulation over one-quarter of the earth's population will be killed by four different means, among which is listed pestilence, indicating a deadly epidemic of some kind that will be sent by God in judgment.

A Summary

To summarize, we have seen that God through Moses warned in Deuteronomy 28 that disobedience to His word would result in a judgment of pestilence. We have seen that from time to time in history God has judged sin with epidemic disease. We have also seen that the Bible prophesies wide spread sexual immorality in the end times and that such depravity will result in a judgment of plagues.

The Sexual Revolution

The Sexual Revolution of the past 30 years has produced the immorality and depravity prophesied in the Bible. And, as promised, the plagues have begun to develop, the most ominous to date being AIDS. Let's look now at the parallels between the current AIDS epidemic and the specific curses which Moses prophesied in Deuteronomy 28.

1) **Deuteronomy 28:16** — "Cursed shall you be in the city, and cursed shall you be in the country." This verse describes the geographic area of the plague and includes both the city and countryside. In other words, the plague is everywhere. It is world wide.

It is estimated that two to three million Americans are

already permanently infected with the AIDS virus, and in many areas of the country the persons infected probably number at least one hundred times those reported as having contracted the full blown syndrome of AIDS. Recently the Center for Disease Control (CDC) in Atlanta released figures that nationwide one out of eighty men are already infected. The number of infected cases is estimated to double every eight to twelve months. More than ten million people are infected in Africa now, where the disease is raging in epidemic and catastrophic proportions. Twenty-one African countries are so devastated they will not report their cases, fearing the stigma of the disease because of its associated homosexuality.

2) **Deuteronomy 28:17** — "Cursed shall be your basket and your kneading bowl." This verse obviously refers to the food supply and the vessels used to collect and utilize the products of the field. One meaning of this verse is that the food supply in the land will be sharply curtailed with resulting famine. This is described in greater detail in verses 18-51. Extreme starvation is described in verses 53-57.

A second way one might interpret these verses is in reference to malnutrition. For example, patients with full blown AIDS syndrome are frequently infected with Cryptosporidiosis — a devastating cholera-like syndrome which produces profuse diarrhea, severe dehydration, nausea, loss of appetite, dramatic weight loss, and malnutrition. This disease appears unremitting and no successful therapy has been identified.

A third way that our food supply might be affected could be related to the fact that the AIDS virus can remain infectious for up to 15 days at room temperature and thus is not as delicate as we would like to think. Transmission through saliva is a theoretical danger, although as yet unproven. If a cook or waiter coughs, or sneezes, or has a cut on the finger, this could theoretically transmit the infection, although no instances of such transmission have yet been documented.

3) **Deuteronomy 28:18** — "Cursed shall be the offspring of your body." If a female infected with the AIDS virus becomes pregnant, there is a 30 to 50 percent chance that the baby will be born infected. The majority of such babies will develop AIDS and die. Pregnancy also affects the mother who is infected, making it more likely that she will develop a full blown AIDS syndrome in a much shorter interval.

Conception by an infected parent entails a substantial risk. In one study which followed fifteen infected pregnant women for thirty months after delivery, 33 percent developed AIDS and 47 percent developed AIDS related complex (ARC), a less severe condition caused by the AIDS virus. In a second study, 45 percent of the mothers developed AIDS or ARC. In addition, one out of three pregnancies delivered a low birth weight infant, and more than half the pregnancies suffered the complication of premature rupture of the membranes with risk of premature delivery and infection. Not only that, but subsequent pregnancies and sibling deliveries were equally complicated, and up to 65 percent of those subsequent infants were infected with AIDS or ARC also. Pregnancy itself apparently makes the mother and the child much more susceptible to the ravages of the AIDS virus.

4) **Deuteronomy 28:19** — "Cursed shall you be when you come in, and cursed shall you be when you go out." The curse is continual, ever present, and involves all the person's daily work and activity. Every place they go and everything they do is cursed.

This could refer to the virus infected secretions. An infected carrier of the virus showing no symptoms is just as capable of spreading AIDS as one that has known infection. This infection is for life, with no way to become "disinfected." The patient is a permanent carrier of the virus. Although spread by coughing has not been proven, the AIDS virus will survive up to fifteen days at room temperature even when dried out, so it is conceivable that coughing or sneezing could present a danger.

A high percentage of adults from Central Africa in later stages of AIDS have pulmonary tuberculosis combined with pulmonary AIDS, known as "CLIP" (Chronic Lymphoid Interstitial Pneumonitis). This is a highly lethal combination since both microbes can be coughed into the air and both can survive more than one week at room temperature outside the body.

5) **Deuteronomy 28:20** — "The Lord will send upon you curses, confusion, and rebuke, in all you undertake to do, until you are destroyed and until you perish quickly, on account of the evil of your deeds, because you have forsaken Me." The word "curses" (in Hebrew, meerah) means a calamity which binds a person with obstacles that render him powerless to resist. The word "confusion" (in Hebrew, mehumah) means panic, severe disturbance or turmoil. The word "rebuke" (in Hebrew, migereth) means frustration or fruitless conclusion of activities. The root word means a

check applied to a person through admonitions or actions.

This last definition is particularly appropriate with respect to infected AIDS patients since they are the "untouchables" of our modern society. Evicted from apartments, fired from their jobs with loss of income, insurance, and even transportation, they are, in effect, ostracized from society.

The phrase "until you perish quickly" is certainly appropriate of AIDS. The incubation period of the disease is slow, but once the symptoms become manifest, death follows quickly. The mean survival time of a full blown AIDS case from the time of diagnosis until death is 18 months.

The phrase, "on account of the evil of your deeds," is particularly appropriate as it relates to AIDS, for the disease has affected mainly three groups — homosexuals, prostitutes and drug addicts. Between 1976 and 1981, AIDS infection was linked almost exclusively in the United States with the practice of homosexuality. Initially called "Gay Related Immunodeficiency Disease," (GRID) the name was changed due to militant homosexual political pressure. In the beginning, 90 percent of AIDS cases in Europe were reported among male homosexuals. In 1985 it was estimated that 70 to 90 percent of practicing homosexuals in San Francisco and New York City were infected. In the African nation of Kenya, more than 50 percent of female prostitutes tested positive for the AIDS virus in 1984. In Miami, Florida, in 1985, more than 41 percent of female prostitutes tested positive. In the United States among urban drug addicted populations, more than 85 percent are infected.

6) **Deuteronomy 28:21** — "The Lord will make the pestilence cling to you until He has consumed you from the land." The word "pestilence" (in Hebrew, deber) means plague or epidemic of some kind, resulting in death. "Cling to you" would indicate that this is a permanent infection and has a very lengthy incubation period. The AIDS virus is classified as a lentivirus, which means it is a slow virus to incubate. Symptoms may develop in a few weeks after infection, but the average incubation time is around five

years. Some infected persons may not show symptoms for
as long as 20 years.

7) **Deuteronomy 28:22** — "The Lord will smite you
with consumption and with fever and with inflammation."
The word "consumption" (in Hebrew, shachepheth)
denotes a wasting disease or a wasting fever. Extreme
weight loss or consumption and fever are characteristics of
the AIDS syndrome. PCP (Pneumocystis Carinii
Pneumonia) and tuberculosis both may cause drenching
night sweats, fever, and extreme weight loss. These are two
of the many "opportunistic infections" which may take
hold once the body's immune systems have been damaged.
Extremely high fever is also typical of cryptococcal men-
ingitis and central nervous system toxoplasmosis, both of
which are frequently seen in AIDS patients.

A recent medical paper reported an alarming epidemic of
central nervous system toxoplasmosis in AIDS victims.
This was described as a lethal intracranial infection. This is
particularly dangerous because 16 to 25 percent of the
population between the ages of 25 and 35 harbor the tox-
oplamsma parasite in the brain or smooth muscle due to exposure to either cat feces or undercooked meat. AIDS allows
proliferation of these organisms. Median survival in these
infections is four months.

The term "inflammation" could denote inflammation of
the liver or colon as well as that of the lungs. Among
homosexual males in San Francisco and New York City, 75
to 90 percent have contracted hepatitis B. In New York
City, San Francisco, and Seattle, 40 percent of male homosexuals who were examined in clinics for sexually transmitted diseases were shown to be infected with both amebiasis
and giardiasis. These two infections, along with a third one
called shigellosis, produce devasting inflammations of the
colon that result in profuse watery diarrhea and rapid
dehydration, all of which are very resistant to treatment.

8) **Deuteronomy 28:27** — "The Lord will smite you with
the boils of Egypt and with tumors and with the scab and
with the itch, from which you cannot be healed." The word
"boils" (in Hebrew, shechin) is misleading in that it does

not indicate what one would think — that is, a staphylococ-
cal skin infection or abscess. Rather, it means an eruption or
inflamed spot. "Scab" (in Hebrew, garab) means itch,
eczema, or skin eruption. The word "itch" (in Hebrew,
cheres) means an eruptive disease. AIDS patients suffer
with many secondary infections, including sexually
transmitted diseases that produce inflamed eruptions of the
skin and scaly skin lesions which itch severely.

The word "tumors" (in Hebrew, ophel) is interesting in
that it has more than one application. The primary meaning
is a tumor, ulcer or swelling. In I Samuel 5:6 & 9 it is stated
that "The hand of the Lord was heavy on the Ashdodites,
and He ravaged them and smote them with tumors . . . and
He smote the men of the city, both young and old, so that
the tumors broke out on them."

The plague described here is similar to the Bubonic
Plague that devastated Europe in the Middle Ages. The
Bubonic Plague or "Black Death" was characterized by
swellings of the lymph glands of the groin and armpits. In
like manner, one of the most noticeable and characteristic
manifestations of AIDS infection is a persistent lym-
phadenopathy or enlargement of lymph nodes throughout
the body.

A secondary meaning of the Hebrew word for "tumor" is
derived from its Arabic root and means "a tumor or boil of
the anus or vulva." It refers to nodes or diseased tissue
located particularly in the rectal area, sometimes referred to
as hemorrhoids in some translations. Homosexual AIDS
patients who are sexually active are plagued by many
lesions involving the rectal and perirectal area (due to rectal
intercourse). The manifestations include inflammatory
psoriasis of the rectum, syphilitic chancre, mucocutaneous
herpes, multiple condylomatalata and anal warts (human
papilloma virus infection).

Both meanings of the Hebrew word for "tumor" are thus
very characteristic of AIDS patients — as manifested in persistent enlargement of the lymph nodes and rectal lesions.

The last phrase of verse 27 states "from which you cannot be healed." At this point in time, there is no known cure

for AIDS and none is on the horizon. This will be discussed in more detail later.

9) **Deuteronomy 28:28** — "The Lord will smite you with madness and with blindness and with bewilderment of heart." The word "bewilderment" (in Hebrew, timmahon) means to be dumbfounded or astonished, with an associated element of fear. Also, it means extreme confusion, even the kind of panic that makes a person powerless. The three curses listed in this verse — madness, blindness, and bewilderment — are characteristic of central nervous system infections with the AIDS virus. It is now known and admitted that the virus invades the brain and destroys cells in the brain, eating it away directly. Irreversible personality changes occur. The patient suffers confusion, depression, memory loss and irrational behavior. Patients frequently have emotional outbursts or panic attacks. Cytomegalovirus or CMV infection produces necrotizing retinitis with resultant blindness.

Ninety percent of AIDS patients have infection of brain tissue which persists for life. The AIDS virus resides and reproduces in cells of the brain. It destroys the cells and produces a progressive, permanent and irreversible loss of memory and loss of muscular control and coordination. It also produces severe psychiatric disturbances, spinal cord degeneration, and brain atrophy or shrinkage. Computerized axial tomography (CAT scan) of the skull shows multiple holes eaten away in the brain tissue, with frequent shrinkage and collapse of the frontal lobes. Also, these patients suffer with seizures, depression, lethargy, confusion, paranoid psychosis with bizarre and aggressive behavior, sudden emotional outbursts, and auditory hallucinations.

10) **Deuteronomy 28:29** — "And you shall grope at noon, as the blind man gropes in darkness, and you shall not prosper in your ways." This verse does not say the person will be blind, but rather that the person will grope about like a blind man gropes in darkness. This means the afflicted will have difficulty with coordination like one who is blind. This, of course, is due to the severe neurological complications and debilitating deterioration of the central

nervous system, as mentioned in the previous paragraph. Those afflicted will be unable to work due to chronic fatigue, chronic illness, and weakness due to loss of muscle mass.

11) **Deuteronomy 28:34** — "And you shall be driven mad by the sight of what you see." The term "mad" or "madness" (in Hebrew, shaga) was covered previously in verse 28. It is interesting that the word means to show abandon or to be demented. "Dementia" is a medical term which characterizes the deterioration of the brain, as described in reference to verse 28. AIDS patients with degeneration of the brain tissue frequently have paranoid delusions and hallucinations. They may feel they have superhuman abilities or, on the contrary, may feel that someone is chasing them and trying to kill them. Emotional outbursts are common.

12) **Deuteronomy 28:35** — "The Lord will strike you on the knees and legs with sore boils, from which you cannot be healed, from the sole of your foot to the crown of your head." The word "sore" (in Hebrew, ra) means bad, evil, deadly and malignant — indicating injurious activity. "Boils" (in Hebrew, shechin), as previously explained, refers to eruptions or inflamed spots. Therefore, "sore boils" means incurable and deadly inflamed spots or eruptions.

The AIDS virus contains five or six genes which are very unstable and may be changing surface characteristics constantly. This characteristic of the virus makes it seem theoretically impossible to develop an effective vaccine. Other lentiviruses show rapid mutation rates and a high degree of dissimilar and unstable gene structures.

Verse 35 is fascinating in that it mentions two different patterns of distribution for the skin lesions. In the first half of the verse it is stated that the Lord will strike the disobedient "on the knees and legs." In the second half of the verse it states that the person will be afflicted from "the sole of the foot to the crown of the head." Among AIDS patients who are almost exclusively homosexual men — for reasons which are unclear — 35 percent are afflicted with a condition known as Kaposi's sarcoma. This is an aggressive skin cancer with multiple purplish spots, splotches, and bumps on the skin surfaces, as well as some internal organs.

Before the discovery of AIDS, the classical form of Kaposi's sarcoma was described in 1872. It was a rare condition, an indolent cancer affecting primarily elderly white males, with lesions confined for the most part to the under side of the buttocks and lower extremities. It was a very slowly progressive condition.

There is now a new and entirely different form of Kaposi's sarcoma that was first observed in 1981. In this form, the distribution of the lesions is from the feet to the head. It is very aggressive and differs from the old classical form not only in occurrence, epidemiology, and clinical features, but also in natural history. Ninety-three percent of the cases in the United States of epidemic Kaposi's sarcoma are found in homosexual or bisexual males, primarily young men.

IN THE WAKE OF CRUSHING DISASTER

THERE ARE AT LEAST 1.5 MILLION PEOPLE IN THE U.S. WHO CARRY THE AIDS VIRUS.

—U.S. NEWS & WORLD REPORT

"GOD IS OUR REFUGE AND STRENGTH, A VERY PRESENT HELP IN TROUBLE." —PSALM 46:1

JACK HAMM

31

This disease, as mentioned, is epidemic and is rapidly progressive with a mean time until death of 18 months. It occurs in three types of skin lesions: 1) a patch of discolored skin; 2) a slightly raised plaque; and 3) an oval nodule. These are dark blue to almost purplish and sometimes brown to almost black in color. These lesions are distributed over the body, frequently on the face, nose, and mouth, as well as the bottoms of the feet. This disease is a sarcoma, a malignant eruption.

13) **Deuteronomy 28:45** — "So all these curses shall come on you and pursue you and overtake you until you are destroyed." A lethal pandemic throughout the crowded cities and villages of the Third World is occurring now and is of a magnitude unparalleled in human history. The AIDS virus will not go away. "These curses **shall** come on you and pursue you and overtake you."

14) **Deuteronomy 28:59** — "Then the Lord will bring extraordinary plagues on you and your descendants, even severe and lasting plagues, and miserable and chronic sicknesses." Many health officials see a frightening effect on world health, which they are powerless to contain. Recently, a study showed 20 to 30 percent of college females tested in some areas of the country were positive for Chlamydia. Chlamydia is a sexually transmitted disease that was only recently introduced into the United States. The AIDS virus can be transmitted in a similar parallel fashion, so obviously the effect on our young women and men could be devastating.

The plague mentioned in Deuteronomy is described as "severe." It is now known that the AIDS retrovirus has extraordinary reproductive capacity. Retroviruses use a special enzyme to convert RNA into DNA. This is the reverse of the classical process of transcription (gene activity) — hence the term, "retrovirus." The virus reproduces rapidly at what has been described as a "ferocious rate." In fact, the level of transcription for the AIDS virus is nothing short of shocking, for it is one thousand times faster than usual genes.

Verse 59 also states that the plagues will be "lasting"

and will be upon "your descendants." Infection with the AIDS retrovirus is a lifetime permanent infection. The AIDS virus incorporates itself into the DNA (genetic material) of infected cells. These integrated viral genes are duplicated with the normal cellular genes so that all future cells will also contain viral genes. Since the viral genes become a part of the permanent genetic material of the host, there is no way to become "disinfected." Keep in mind that these lentiviruses, as mentioned, have a very long asymptomatic latent period. These two factors — a long latent period and self-perpetuation — ensure that this plague will continue on through our descendents and will not burn out. This is an entirely different situation from plagues of the past, in that they were not due to lentiviruses. Keep in mind that **this is the first human lentivirus infection ever recorded.**

Verse 59 also states that the plagues will be "miserable and chronic sicknesses." This is a quite obvious description of AIDS from what we have considered thus far. However, there is another aspect of the problem, and that is the staggering economic impact. AIDS patients are for the most part unable to care for themselves. Forty percent are brain impaired. At this time the cost for caring for an AIDS patient is estimated to be between $50,000 and $150,000 per patient, assuming an average survival time from diagnosis to death of 18 months. It is estimated that in four years the cost for total care of patients will be sixteen billion dollars. Under these circumstances, health insurance companies will go bankrupt. Our health care system will be in shambles and will finally collapse under the load. Our Social Security programs, due to the disability classification of AIDS patients, will be totally depleted.

15) **Deuteronomy 28:61** — "Also every sickness and every plague which, not written in the book of this law, the Lord will bring on you until you are destroyed." This verse speaks of diseases not recorded — in other words, new diseases. The AIDS retrovirus is unique and was isolated only in 1984. Some speculate that it may have mutated from a primate retrovirus found in the African green monkey. It

may have invaded the United States as early as 1970, but due to the lengthy incubation period, cases resembling AIDS were not seen until about 1976. These cases were reported to the CDC in 1981 but not identified until 1984 when the virus was actually isolated.

16) **Deuteronomy 28:62** — "Then you shall be left few in number, whereas you were as the stars of the heaven for multitude." Although at this time it is estimated that 30 percent of those infected will develop the actual AIDS syndrome over a five year period, several experts anticipate that the vast majority of those infected will over the next five to ten years or even longer develop life threatening illnesses.

Concluding Thoughts

God takes no pleasure in placing judgments upon us for sin. He has no choice but to do so, for He is perfectly holy and righteous, and He therefore must deal with sin. He is also a God of love, and He would not be loving if He allowed sin to go unpunished.

We can be thankful that He never judges without warning. He has warned us about the consequences of sin in His Word. And throughout history He has raised up prophetic voices who stood on His Word and called people to repentance. He does not desire that any should perish (II Peter 3:9). He always warns before He judges. And even when He inflicts judgment, His primary purpose is to prompt repentance:

The Lord is compassionate and gracious,
Slow to anger and abounding in lovingkindness.
(Psalm 103:8)

The Lord is slow to anger and great in power,
And the Lord will by no means leave the guilty
unpunished.
(Nahum 1:3)

From the beginning of time Man has sought to defy God's laws and not suffer the consequences. Man has never succeeded. The Sexual Revolution constitutes blatant rebellion against God and His Word. The Revolution is now reaping its harvest. God is patient, but He will not be mocked (Gal. 6:7).

LOOKING TO THE FUTURE
By Dr. David R. Reagan

Is there any hope for our society? It depends on where you look for a solution. The world says the only hope is "safe sex." The world's "savior" is the condom.

SAFEGUARD AGAINST AIDS

PREMARITAL CONTINENCE AND FAITHFUL RELATIONSHIP AFTER MARRIAGE. "THE TWO SHALL BE ONE FLESH." — EPH. 5:31

Safe Sex or Moral Sex?

The world's solution is no solution at all. It will compound the disaster. Pushing the condom simply encourages promiscuous sex. And the condom is not all that effective. Keep in mind that the condom is effective only 90% of the time in preventing pregnancy, even though a pregnancy can occur only two or three days out of a month. The transmission of AIDS can occur with *every* sex act on *any* day of the month. When an unwanted pregnancy occurs, abortion can serve as a back up means of escape. There is no escape from AIDS. When it is contracted, it ultimately means death. Relying on a condom is like playing Russian roulette.

The only valid hope for stemming the AIDS epidemic is to be found in the Bible. God's Word makes it clear that our hope is not "safe sex" but, rather, moral sex. Sexual union within marriage with one faithful partner is the only way to be sexually active and free from the danger of AIDS.

The world calls such a solution "square." The Bible presents it as God's perfect plan for Man. This means the Church must proclaim the whole sexual revolution to be a sin against God and must call our nation to repentance, while preaching the good news that in Christ there is the power to be set free from bondage to any sexual sin.

"Moralizing"

The world says such a "moralizing approach" will never work. "People are going to fornicate anyway," says the world. Yes, but that doesn't mean that government has to endorse and encourage it by handing them a condom.

But what is so "moralizing" about advocating proper behavior? We do it in every other area of life. We tell people they can't steal money or loot houses or kill other people. We pass laws against such behavior and prescribe stiff penalties. No one shouts, "Moralizing!" No one says we should not have such laws because people will go ahead and embezzle, burglarize and murder.

Why is the sexual area of life so different, particularly when the improper behavior threatens the very existence of society with deadly disease? The very ones who shout,

"Moralizing!" when it comes to sex, are the very same ones who moralize with great fervor when it comes to wearing a seat belt or killing whales or smoking in public.

And speaking of smoking, the anti-smoking campaign in this country is a classic example of the effectiveness of moralizing an issue. Since the Surgeon General's report in the 60's, the number of people smoking in our society has dropped from a majority to less than 30%. Much if not most of this decline has been due to both public and private campaigns to picture smoking as socially unacceptable.

Or what about the current national antidrug campaign? Its focal point is a slogan: "Just say no!" The liberals have not denounced that as "moralizing." Yet they would scream to high heaven if someone were to suggest that the same slogan be used in a campaign to curb promiscuous sex among teenagers. When it comes to sex, we can't even suggest that kids say "No!" Rather, we tell them, "Play it safe — use a condom." What sick logic!

The Christian Agenda

We as Christians need to be the salt of the earth and the light of the world by standing for righteousness on the issue of AIDS. To do so, we must speak out boldly and unashamedly in behalf of God's Word:

1) Stressing chastity for the unmarried;

2) Emphasizing fidelity for the married; and

3) Demanding quarantine for the infected.

The very mention of the word "quarantine" elicits cries of injustice and accusations of being merciless. But quarantine is a time honored and proven method of dealing with infectious diseases. It was one of the keys to breaking the spread of the plague in Europe in the Middle Ages. It was used extensively in this country at the turn of the century to quell the tuberculosis epidemic when thousands of people were placed in sanitariums.

I was placed in quarantine in a special hospital ward when I was a child. I had a virulent intestional infection. It was not deadly, like AIDS. But it was serious, and it was infectious. My younger brother was placed in quarantine when he came down with scarlet fever. I remember it vividly because he was kept at home, and the medical authorities placed large signs on our house warning people to stay away. Quarantine is also a Biblical approach to dealing with disease. In Leviticus 13 & 14 and Numbers 5, God commanded that lepers be made to live outside the camp or the city. He also directed that any house where a person developed leprosy had to be quarantined and cleansed before anyone else could live in it.

Quarantine is not merciless. It is an act of mercy toward society. It is an act of tough love toward the one who is quarantined. And tough love is precisely what is needed in dealing with a disease like AIDS. We need to show compassion toward those with AIDS, providing them with the best medical care possible and sharing the Gospel with them. But they must also be made to face up to the reality and danger of their disease and the unwillingness of society to tolerate the immoral and illegal lifestyles of homosexuality and drug abuse that produce 95% of the cases.

There is a difference in compassion and sentimentality. Thus far, the reaction to AIDS has been characterized by a sort of befuddled sentimentality that makes heroes out of people like Rock Hudson and Liberace. People like these are not heroes. Nor are they martyrs. They are people who experienced tragic deaths because they lived in rebellion against God. To make heroes out of them is to encourage others to emulate their rebellion.

Effective quarantine will require compulsory blood testing for the entire population. Again, the mention of blood tests raises cries of "injustice" and "civil rights." But these cries are misplaced. What about the rights of those who do not want to get infected? Doesn't society have a right to protect itself? We presently require compulsory smallpox vaccinations. What's the difference? The difference, of course, is that one test threatens the sexual revolution whereas the other does not.

The Key To Survival

In II Chronicles 7:14 God gave Solomon the formula for national survival:

> If my people who are called by My Name will humble themselves and pray, and seek My face and turn from their wicked ways, then will I hear from heaven and forgive their sins and heal their land.

That statement means that the fate of our nation is in the hands of Christians — "those who are called by My name." Are we willing to fall on our faces before God, repent of our sins and the sins of our nation, and call out to God for mercy?

I doubt it. As Paul prophesied in II Timothy 3:5, Christendom today in the United States "has the form of religion but has denied its power." We have sold out to a Pollyanna Gospel of health, wealth and power that has put us in bed with the world. Instead of pointing people to the blood of Christ and calling them to repentance and lives of self-denial, we talk about positive confession, self-esteem, and ego gratification.

Our pulpits are silent about the moral issues that are destroying us. We are murdering 5,000 babies a day in the name of freedom of choice for women, and hardly a whimper is heard from the pulpit. We are drowning in a sea of pornography while our preachers expound the glories of prosperity. Our children are corrupted and enslaved by satanic music, but from the pulpits come only the sounds of silence.

Christendom has lost its spiritual sensitivity. Its moral conscience has become calloused. It has become too much a part of the world for it to speak to the world.

Meanwhile, our government has been taken over by secular humanists who are determined to destroy the fundamental principles of Judaeo-Christian ethics — the very principles that made this nation great.

40

Looking to the Future

I fear we have gone too far down the path of immorality. It has become ingrained in our national character — or lack thereof.

The wrath of God hangs over our heads. It has fallen on the homosexual community. It is falling on the house of God, for judgment always begins in God's family. Soon, it will fall on our whole nation. We are living on borrowed time.

NEW PUBLICATIONS FROM LAMB & LION

Study Guide

The Christ in Prophecy Study Guide is a letter-sized, spiral bound book of 135 pages. It contains a listing of every Messianic prophecy in the Bible concerning both the First and Second Advents of the Lord. All the prophecies are analytically organized by topic.

The first section of the guide is devoted to a detailed listing of the First Coming prophecies, giving both their source and their fulfillment. The Second Coming prophecies are grouped into four categories: the Law, the Prophets, the Psalms, and the New Testament. Each section has an introductory essay at the beginning and a detailed index at the end.

This book is the culmination of seven years of prophetic study and research by Dr. Reagan. You will find it to be an invaluable tool for the study of God's Prophetic Word. The cost is $10.

Mail your order to:

Lamb & Lion Ministries
P. O. Box K
McKinney, TX 75069

Learning to Walk by Faith

Dr. David Reagan

Trusting God is the story of Dr. Reagan's wrestling match with God and how he learned through that struggle to walk by faith. Using a light hearted, anecdotal approach, Dr. Reagan takes a look at the basic issues of everyday Christian living and identifies the key principles for walking by faith.

Dr. Reagan addresses many crucial questions which confront Christians daily: Does God still perform miracles? Does the Holy Spirit still give spiritual gifts? Does God still provide direct guidance? Is the Bible relevant to our problems? Is there power in prayer? Are we living in the end times?

It is a moving book that will have you laughing one moment and crying the next. A paperback of 190 pages costing $7.

Mail your order to:

Lamb & Lion Ministries
P. O. Box K
McKinney, TX 75069

NEW STUDY RESOURCE FROM LAMB & LION

An Overview of Revelation is a study packet that consists of an album of 12 cassette tapes and a 60 page spiral bound study guide. Each tape is one hour long. The tapes and study guide cover the entire book of Revelation, chapter by chapter. Dr. Reagan is the speaker on the tapes. He is also the author of the study guide.

Dr. Reagan believes that the book of Revelation was meant to be understood and that it can be understood by any spirit-led Christian. Dr. Reagan's approach is to accept the Revelation story for its plain sense meaning.

This study packet can be used individually or in groups. The album and study guide sell for $25. Separate study guides cost $5 each.

Mail your order to:

**Lamb & Lion Ministries
P. O. Box K
McKinney, TX 75069**